I0479971

© **Copyright 2023 - All rights reserved.**

All rights reserved. No part of this guide may be reproduced, transmitted, or distributed in any form or by any means without permission in writing from the publisher except in the case of brief quotations embodied in critical articles or reviews.

Legal & Disclaimer

The content and information in this book is consistent and truthful, and it has been provided for informational, educational and business purposes only.

The content and information contained in this book has been compiled from reliable sources, which are accurate based on the knowledge, belief, expertise and information of the Author.

R Social Publishing

www.thesocialr.com

Table of Contents

Foreword

In 1885, persecution and massacre of Christians in Lebanon led my paternal great-grandfather to exile in the United States. After 25 years, he returned to his native land, the village of Souk El Gharb, located in Mount Lebanon. The village was the center of sales of agricultural products from the surrounding villages. He had bought the rights to the market; any merchant had to pay him to have access to a sales location. The tax was 10% of sales. My grandfather and his younger brother were in charge of collecting payments from merchants for things that were sometimes not so simple. Some situations ended in fights!

My paternal grandfather left Lebanon by boat for Liberia, Monrovia. My maternal grandmother was not able to study; she was born in Goma in the DRC. Her mother died when she was still a baby. She grew up alongside her father, who had a business and spent her days there. At the age of 14, her father left her. She was married by force after the death of her father. A marriage obviously catastrophic where she quickly understood that she had to be financially independent. Goma was full of foreigners. She discovered that the cigar was very popular, so she made it her first business. Without reading or writing, she was one of the first car importers from Europe to the DRC and then embarked on various businesses, opened a paint production plant, and invested in real estate. She has more than ensured her retirement!

Examples among others of people who undertook and succeeded in unlikely situations and, in the case of my grandmother, without reading or writing. So, I ask you, what do you want to do with your life? You can succeed, nothing can stop you except yourself.

Introduction

1991, in the car I sang "lokuta munene lokuta munene", it is a song I learned at school. I was a student at the chicks, a small building located in the center of Kinshasa. That day my mother, brother, and I were going to the airport. The civil war forced us to leave the country and put an end to our family life. I was eight years old when we arrived in Belgium as a refugee; advantaged by financial means, our material situation was rather comfortable. This war had divided our family, and my father for work had to stay. At this precise moment, the words war, obligation, work, and money took on meaning in my subconscious and marked a long series of trauma.

My father was divided between Kinshasa (DRC) and Monrovia (Liberia), two unstable countries. As his business was there, he could not help but dedicate himself to it. So we grew up without him with the background of conversation: "I can't come, I work for you, I'm blocked by the war ... »
These words had an impressive impact on my life. My studies were for me an opportunity to learn, learn as much as possible, and store knowledge to go quickly to work and free my father from the war.
At 16, I started student jobs where I worked as a saleswoman in a home object store, an evening served in a bar where I was asked to sit after the second service as I was not talented in punctual events as a hostess, but I was able to acquire knowledge in communication, sales, and public relations. It was such an interesting time.

In March 2010, I landed in Angola after one year of adaptation to the country. I decided to open my construction, renovation, and interior design company. It was a real challenge filled with challenges every day, the search for materials and skilled workers. The construction sites were purgatories for the soul. I learned patience, respect for others, and sharing knowledge. I had become an electrician, plumber, tiler, and mason in six months. The work was a team effort to provide customers with quality construction. The original meaning of the word "to serve others" was well established.

In 2016, an economic crisis hit Angola; Brent (oil prices) had gone from 130 to 30, which did not cover the cost of production of a barrel. Angola depended on more than 90% of oil revenue, which was its main source. So, we went back to the census and the world of construction slowed down. It was necessary to quickly find an alternative, a business that would allow me to hold during this time. The food; everyone needs to nest themselves, so I turned to the world of catering: Provide cheap food.

While undertaking this field, I realized the impact that food importation had on our daily lives. Rising commodity prices, shortages of certain foods, and our dependence on imports were simply unacceptable and totally incomprehensible! How have we managed to get to this point? Seeing the population running out of more and more food was staggering for a country with fertile land where we still find nourishing forests abundant in fruits and vegetables but little known and unexploited. I was a spectator of an abusive economic operation that had reached my fridge: Empty, it was most of the time! The difficulties in feeding my children made me aware of the social difficulties of the population. This real shock reinforced in me the desire to put in place solutions for a viable change. And this involved the creation of business; the economic development of the country is essential, provided that priorities are reviewed: food, housing, education, and health care. These areas of activity are more than essential to set up, and for that, it takes ENTREPRENEURS!!!

Entrepreneurship refers to the action of undertaking or carrying out a project. The term entrepreneurship means creating an (economic) activity to achieve a goal to meet a need. The creator represents the entrepreneur, the project leader.

The etymology of the word entrepreneur is 'inter prehendere' from Latin, which means to grasp with the hand. The word "prehendere" means "to grasp" to take to master, differently from the verb "capere" meaning to seize with the notion of seizing oneself, to capture.

It is said that speech has power. The meaning of each word used must be known. Outside our days, we do not look for the origin of words; we use them without knowing their meaning and value.

Today a good number of people embark on entrepreneurship without understanding the primary meaning of this activity. Behind the production machine of "entrepreneurs" hides real entrepreneurs who explode the lack of knowledge of people hungry for immediate wealth.
We are in an era where we want to make a lot of money effortlessly. There is no more creativity. We have become machines to copy, consume, throw away, and all this at a frightening speed. We always want more, faster, and cheaper.

But our mode of operation can no longer last because it impacts humanity as a whole. Did you know that to make a cabinet from a discount brand, the pieces can come from 5 different countries? Imports are constantly growing all over the world. It is the same principle for a cheap brand jacket: fabrics, buttons, pull-pull, etc., are purchased in different countries and then assembled and sent to countries around the world.
Commercial vessels are the most polluting transport in the world. It uses the worst fuel, which remains once the other petroleum products have been refined, a viscous residue of oil, heavy and difficult to burn. It is estimated that a container ship pollutes as many as 50 million cars!

We have become responsible for the exploitation of cheap labor, for wars killing several million people in areas where raw materials indispensable for the development of humanity are to be found, for enriching a group of people who have the financial means to manipulate the world in their favor; so, the rich see themselves even richer, and the works sink. It is not inevitable, but it is important that we get to this point for general awareness and act by taking note of new perspectives.

Here we will see together the basics of entrepreneurship and what you need to know to decide whether to start an economic activity.

Chapter 1: CANVAS

Just a reminder:

At the most basic economic level, a business model is a logic with which an organization ensures its financial viability. Put simply, how an organization intends to make money.

Here we will see the Canvas business model.

The canvas template was created by the Swiss Alexander Osterwalder to facilitate the strategic planning of new companies in a fast and agile way.

It is the replacement of the business plan to present a business model and its competitive advantages. The canvas business plan is visual and synthetic. Its playful aspect allows you to quickly set up a plan in 9 points and on a single page, while the business plan is a booklet of several dozen pages. However, the business canvas remains limited because it does not address market research and focuses on a type of clientele. So, for each client, a canvas.

The business model canvas is divided into 9 key questions:

BUSINESS MODEL CANVAS

KEY PARTNERS	KEY ACTIVITIES	VALUE PROPOSITION	CUSTOMER RELATIONSHIPS	CUSTOMER SEGMENTS
	KEY RESOURCES		CHANNELS	
COST STRUCTURE		REVENUE STREAMS		

- **Key partners**: are the people, organizations, and companies that can help your company do what it needs to do.

Partnerships can be:
I.   strategic alliances between two companies that are **not competing** to deliver a better service or make themselves known;
II.   strategic alliances between two companies **competing** to join forces;

Partnerships can have different reasons for existing:
I.   **Optimize and save money:** the buyer-supplier relationship is sometimes easier to optimize a business. It is often counterproductive for a company to own all the resources or to carry out each activity itself.

Partnerships that allow optimization and economies of scale are, therefore, essential to reduce costs.

II.   **Reduce risk and uncertainty:** In a competitive environment, it is possible to ally in one area while continuing to compete in another.

- **Key activities:** describes the most important physical or intellectual actions your company needs to take to create value in its business. These are activities where continuous training and knowledge are key elements of success. Key activities can be categorized:

I.   **Make** it happen: Manufacture products, design/develop/deliver services and solve problems. For service companies, "doing" can refer to both the preparation of the future service and the service itself.

II.   **Sell**: Promote, publicize, or educate customers about the value of the service or product. (Commercial calls, planning or deployment of advertising campaigns or promotions, and awareness or training.

III. **Problem-solving**: Developing new solutions that solve customer problems.

IV.   **Support**: Contributes to the smooth running of the organization but is not directly associated with "doing" or "selling" (recruiting employees, keeping accounts, or other administrative tasks)

- **Key** resources: all assets essential to the operation of the company. The resources are:

Physical resources: Land, buildings, machinery, and vehicles are essential elements in many business models.

Intellectual resources: Intangible elements such as trademarks, systems, and methods developed by the company, software, patents, and intellectual property rights.

Human resources: include all staff in the broad sense; entrepreneurs, employees, partners, and volunteers necessary for the production and sale of the goods and/or services composing the offer.

Financial resources: Liquidity, lines of credit or financial guarantees, etc.

Key partners, key resources, and key activities are the three components that respond to each other on an ongoing basis. If one of these components fails, it can have serious consequences on the company's production capacity.

Study and analyze the internal environment of the partners (their histories, lifelines, the constituent parts of their business models, their results, etc.). The information that will help you choose the best partners.

- **Value proposition**: this is a statement that accurately and clearly describes the value you will bring to your users through your idea. This is

The Value Proposition Canvas

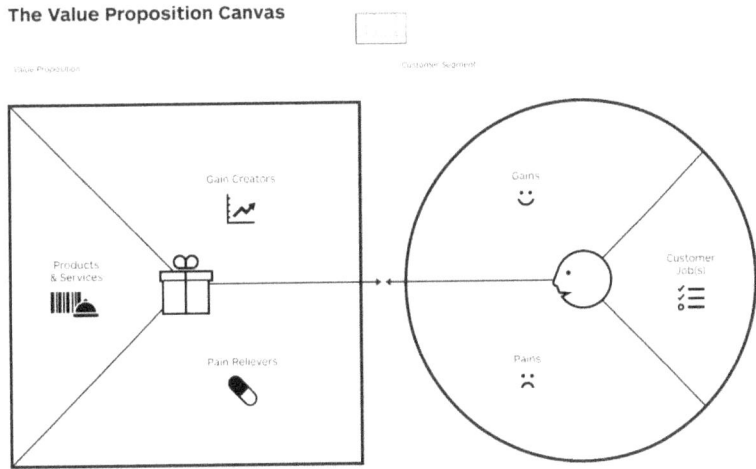

why customers will buy your goods and services rather than that of a competitor. Writing your value proposition is a step that requires hindsight and can be difficult. The value proposition canvas is a simple, concrete, and quick tool to implement. It helps you develop and manage your value proposition:

1. Define your customer base: Know who you serve, and understand what motivates them.

2. Match benefits to customer needs: As you build your value proposition, think about how your offerings solve their problems and help them achieve their ambitions.
3. Communicate accurately, using numbers or percentages.
4. Don't be afraid to be unique in a fast-paced world; where competition is tough. You have to mark your difference and be original while knowing your customers' needs perfectly.
5. Test your value proposition.

Note: Your users do not buy your products for the "how" (How does it work? What features?)
More for the "why."

        - What are our values?

        ....

        ....

        ....

        ....

        ....

        ....

        ....

        ....

        ....

        ....

        - Our engines?

....
....

....
....

....
....

....
....

....
....

- Why do we do ?

....
....

....
....

....
....

....
....

....
....

- **Customer relations: CUSTOMERS ARE AT THE HEART OF YOUR PROJECT.** The **relationships** you will maintain with your **customers** are an integral part of your business model. You need to think about how you are going to communicate with them. There are several steps before someone becomes your customer:

- Before purchase - considered to be a prospect; at this stage, the company must be noticed by the prospect.
- During purchase - a customer, the company must trigger the act of purchase.
- After buying - Has become a user, and the company must optimize the experience and encourage him to spread the brand.

To identify the types of customer relationships to set up, you can ask yourself these questions:

- What relationship does each customer segment want us to establish and maintain?

....
....
....
....
....
....
....
....
....
....

- What relationship have we set up?

....
....
....
....
....
....
....
....
....
....

- How are these customer relationships integrated into the business model canvas?

....
....
....
....
....
....
....
....
....
....

- How much do they cost?

....
....

....
....

....
....

....
....

....
....

....
....

The different types of customer relations are:

1. **Individual service**: The customer is in direct contact with company personnel. It can be a phone call, an email, or even a face-to-face exchange. This service aims to accompany and advise the customer for a purchase or a delivery or to ensure the after-sales service.
2. **Individual service dedicates** this is the same type of customer relationship as individual service, with the big difference that the customer benefits from a contact person specifically for him. For example, banks for their wealthy clients.
3. **Self-service**: The company sets up the necessary so that the customer can buy without outside help; no direct relationship is established with the customer.
4. **Service automates**: the automated service takes the basics of self-service but has the particularity of adapting to customer needs. An online store is an example.
5. **Communities**: this type of relationship makes it possible to create customer communities and therefore retain them
6. **Co-creation**: this type of customer relationship goes beyond simply exchanging with your customer base; it is also about involving them in value creation. Like platforms that ask customers to write their reviews of a product.

- **Distribution channels:** are created so that companies can answer the question: "how do we get our products to the consumer?"

1. Offline channels: those that do not go through the Internet, TV, radio ... to contact their customers. example, the traditional physical store
2. Online channels: web-based
- **Customer segments**: Segmentation consists of classifying your customers according to different criteria and creating different groups of homogeneous customers. The greater the number of criteria taken into account, the more precise the targeting can be.

The three criteria to know to segment your customer base:
- **The criteria of a sociodemographic nature** are the simplest and most obvious. This involves classifying customers based on their social status, age, gender, etc.

We can distinguish three types of socio demographic criteria:
- Socio-economic criteria: occupation, socio-professional category, income level.
- Demographic criteria: age, sex, family situation, marital status, level of education, height, and weight.
- Geographical criteria: the place of residence, place of work

- **Criteria of a psychological nature:** Here, we are interested in the personality of the customer, for example:
- Lifestyle
- Activities
- Hobbies and interests
- Opinions

        Psychological criteria are harder to obtain, but they are insightful for marketing.

Behavioral criteria can be linked:
- To the purchasing situation: does the customer buy occasionally or frequently?

- The benefits that the customer seeks through his purchases
- The degree of customer loyalty
- Purchasing behavior: means of payment used, delivery method, purchase period

For a relevant analysis, you must cross-segmentations. Purely socio demographic criteria are not enough; they must be accompanied by psychological or behavioral criteria.

Chapter 2: VISION

The word "vision" comes from the Latin word "visio," which means "act of seeing." It refers to both the physical act of seeing and the mental act of conceiving or imagining. The quote "A people without vision is a people who perish" is from the Bible and highlights the importance of having a clear direction or purpose in life, without which people can become lost or stagnant. This quote is relevant not only for individuals but also for families, organizations, and companies. It emphasizes the importance of having a clear vision and a plan for the future to achieve success and fulfillment.

A company's vision is a projection into the future, representing the change you want to create.
Having a clear vision is important not only for companies but also for individuals and families. Without a clear direction, making progress and achieving meaningful goals can be difficult. A clear vision helps to establish a sense of purpose and meaning, providing a roadmap for where we want to go and how we plan to get there. It can help to prioritize decisions, guide behavior, and provide motivation and inspiration. In entrepreneurship, having a clear vision can help set a company apart, attract customers and investors, and provide a sense of direction and focus for employees, individuals, and families.

From a young age, we are often given orders and told what to do. We are expected to attend school, get good grades, and eventually pursue higher education or a career. While these goals may be important, others often establish them, and we may not have a clear sense of our own direction or purpose. As a result, many become dependent on others for guidance, asking for advice on major life decisions or relying on external factors such as social norms or peer pressure to guide their behavior.

This lack of a clear personal vision can lead to a sense of aimlessness or unfulfillment, as we may not pursue the things that truly matter to us. In entrepreneurship, this can be particularly problematic, as the business's success may depend on the entrepreneur's ability to establish a clear vision and take decisive action to achieve their goals. It's important, therefore, for individuals to take the time to develop their own vision for their life and career rather than relying solely on the goals and expectations of others. Doing so can establish a clear sense of purpose and direction and make decisions aligned with their values and goals.

Vision is a clear plan that will allow you to anticipate. A good leader must know where and how she is going.
Vision is a management tool that makes it possible to:
- Create the conditions for sustainable and sustainable performance
- Mobilize teams
- Prepare for the future
- Master change

These two questions will allow you to define your vision:
How can you make a difference in this world?

....
....
....
....
....
....
....
....
....
....

Why is it important?

....
....

....
....

....
....

....
....

....
....

To answer it you must rely on two pillars:

1.   Uninhibited, you must have crazy confidence in yourself! Don't compare yourself to what already exists. You are an entrepreneur to bring something more to the world.

2.   Identify your theme:

What are you passionate about?

....
....

....
....

....
....

....
....

....
....

What questions do you constantly ask yourself?

....
....

....
....
....
....
....
....
....
....

-       What are your strengths?

....
....
....
....
....
....
....
....
....
....

There is no small vision. Vision evolves, and it adapts. The main thing is to start because you will have to modify it according to the permanent change our world is experiencing today.

For example, artificial intelligence (AI) has entered the offices of some companies to perform administrative tasks, which was still a dream ten years ago. They can now learn on their own and take up human intellectual jobs.

AI has become essential in all sectors; it is an obligation that is difficult to escape. Before long, AI will be everyone's business. Companies not aware of the urgency of integrating AI may well disappear from the business landscape. Formulating a vision will always be useful whether you are a business owner, department manager or freelancer. Your vision will carry the change you want to create.

A Company's Vision

A company represents the change the company wants to create. A company's vision is a statement that describes the company's long-term aspirations and the impact it hopes to make on the world. It serves as a guide for decision-making and provides a sense of direction and purpose for the organization.

A company's vision should be inspiring and ambitious, capturing the imagination of employees and stakeholders and motivating them to work towards a common goal. It should be clear, concise, and easy to understand so that it can be easily communicated to others.

A well-crafted vision can significantly impact a company's success, helping to align employees and stakeholders around a common goal and providing a clear focus for the organization. It can also serve as a powerful marketing tool, helping differentiate the company from its competitors and attracting customers who share its values and aspirations.

Ultimately, a company's vision should be more than just a statement on paper - it should be a living, breathing part of the company's culture, guiding decision-making and shaping the organization's strategic direction.

A powerful management tools

A clear vision can also serve as a powerful management tool, providing various benefits for the organization. These benefits include:

Creating the conditions for sustainable and sustainable performance: A clear vision provides a sense of direction and purpose for the organization, helping to align employees and stakeholders around a common goal. This can improve performance and productivity as everyone works towards a shared vision.

Mobilizing teams: A well-crafted vision can inspire and motivate employees, creating a sense of ownership and pride in their work. This can lead to improved teamwork and collaboration, as everyone works towards a common goal.

Preparing for the future: A clear vision provides a roadmap for the organization's future, helping to anticipate changes and challenges that may lie ahead. This can help the organization to be proactive rather than reactive, making strategic decisions that will position it for long-term success.

Mastering change: A clear vision can provide stability and continuity during change or uncertainty. It can help to guide decision-making and ensure that the organization stays true to its values and goals, even in the face of external pressures or shifting priorities.

Why is vision important in conscious entrepreneurship?

Vision is important in conscious entrepreneurship for several reasons:
Vision sets the direction: A clear and compelling vision provides a roadmap for the business, setting out where it wants to go and how it plans to get there. This direction helps the business to focus its efforts, resources, and strategies in a way that aligns with its long-term goals.

Vision inspires action: A well-crafted vision can inspire and motivate entrepreneurs, employees, and other stakeholders to take action towards achieving the vision. This inspiration can help to create a culture of innovation, creativity, and commitment to the business's mission and goals.

Vision motivates stakeholders: A shared vision can be a powerful motivator for stakeholders, including employees, investors, customers, and partners. When everyone is working towards a common goal, they are more likely to feel a sense of ownership and engagement in the business's success.

Vision enhances decision-making: A clear vision can help guide decision-making, making it easier to prioritize and allocate resources in a way that aligns with the business's long-term goals. This clarity can help entrepreneurs and managers to make tough decisions with confidence and purpose.

Vision creates a sense of purpose and meaning: A strong vision can create a sense of purpose and meaning for everyone involved in the business. This sense of purpose can help to foster a deeper connection to the business's mission and values, creating a sense of pride and commitment among stakeholders.

Overall, a well-crafted vision can help to create a sense of direction, purpose, and motivation for the business and its stakeholders, guiding decision-making and inspiring action towards achieving its long-term goals.

How to Develop a Vision in Conscious Entrepreneurship?

Developing a clear and compelling vision is critical for conscious entrepreneurs who want to create positive change in the world. Here are some key steps to developing a vision:

Reflect on personal values: Start by reflecting on your values and what motivates you as an entrepreneur. What do you care about? What inspires you? What do you want to achieve with your business? You can develop a vision that aligns with your passions and purpose by connecting with your personal values.

Analyze market trends and customer needs: It's important to understand your industry's market trends and customer needs. What are the current and emerging trends? What are your customers looking for? By understanding the market, you can develop a relevant and responsive vision for your customers' needs.

Consider the impact on society and the environment: Conscious entrepreneurship is about creating a positive impact in the world. As you develop your vision, consider the impact that your business can have on society and the environment. How can you create value for your customers while positively contributing to the world?

Engage stakeholders in the visioning process: Developing a vision is not a solo endeavor. Engaging your stakeholders, including employees, partners, customers, and community members, is important in the visioning process. By involving others, you can get diverse perspectives and ideas that can help shape your vision and build buy-in and commitment.

Use storytelling to convey the vision: Use storytelling to convey your vision compellingly. Use metaphors, analogies, and vivid language to paint a picture of the future you want to create. Tell a story that inspires and motivates your stakeholders to join you on the journey.

CHAPTER 3: VALUE

The etymology of the word value is Valor from Latin, "quality of a person who makes him worthy of esteem" A high-performance team shares common values. A company's values are the principles on which it bases itself to evolve in its sector and make its strategic decisions. The values of a company represent the vision of its leader; they allow him to set goals, make the right decisions on a daily basis, position itself in its market, and stand out from the competition. Below are some values that successful entrepreneurs have.

Excellence

As a conscious entrepreneur, you should strive for excellence in everything you do. Aim for the highest possible standard in all aspects of your business, from the products and services you offer to the customer experience you provide. To be excellent, you need to be committed to continuous learning, growth, and improvement. This means staying up-to-date with the latest industry trends, investing in ongoing training and development, and seeking feedback from customers and employees to identify areas for improvement.

Your focus on the customer is paramount. As you prioritize excellence, you should put the needs and wants of your customers at the center of everything you do. Take the time to understand your customers' pain points, needs, and desires, and then work tirelessly to develop products and services that meet or exceed those expectations. Go above and beyond to provide exceptional customer service, take ownership of mistakes and make things right, and always strive to exceed expectations.

Paying attention to detail is also essential. As you prioritize excellence, you understand that the little things matter. You should pay close attention to every aspect of your business, from the design and packaging of your products to the wording of your marketing messages. You understand that even the smallest detail can make a big difference in how your business is perceived by customers and can be the deciding factor in whether a customer chooses to do business with you or not.

Finally, your commitment to integrity and ethical business practices is vital. As you prioritize excellence, you understand that your reputation is everything and that your success is built on a foundation of trust with your customers and employees. Make a conscious effort to operate your business with transparency and honesty, to treat your employees with respect and fairness, and to give back to the communities you serve.

Trust

As a conscious entrepreneur, you should prioritize trust in your business. Trust is built on a foundation of reliability, credibility, and confidence between you and your stakeholders. To build trust, you need to prioritize honesty, transparency, consistency, empathy, respect, and accountability in your actions and communication.

Honesty and transparency are essential components of building trust. You should be open and honest with your customers, employees, and partners, communicate clearly and straightforwardly, and be transparent about your business practices, policies, and financial situation. This level of honesty and transparency builds credibility and reliability, which fosters a sense of trust among stakeholders.

Consistency is another key component of building trust. You should maintain a consistent level of quality in your products and services, and you should always deliver on your promises. You should meet deadlines, honor contracts, and always deliver what you say you will. By being consistent, you demonstrate reliability, which is crucial for building trust.

In addition to honesty, transparency, and consistency, trust requires empathy and respect for others. You should show empathy and respect for your customers, employees, and partners. Take the time to listen to their needs and concerns and treat them with respect, dignity, and fairness, which builds a sense of trust and goodwill.

Trust is also about taking responsibility for your actions. You should take responsibility for your mistakes and work to make things right. Be accountable for your actions and take steps to rebuild trust when it has been broken. Strive to improve your processes and practices to prevent mistakes from happening again in the future.

Team spirit

As a conscious entrepreneur, it's important to value team spirit in your business. Team spirit is about fostering a sense of community, collaboration, and support among your employees. By cultivating team spirit, you can create a more engaged, motivated, and productive workforce that can help you achieve your business goals.

To foster team spirit, you should encourage communication, collaboration, and mutual support among your employees. Create a positive work environment where everyone feels welcome, respected, and valued. Encourage open communication and feedback, and make sure that everyone has a voice and an opportunity to contribute.

Set clear goals and objectives for your team, and make sure that everyone understands their roles and responsibilities. Encourage your team to work together to achieve these goals, and reward collaboration and teamwork. Celebrate team successes and acknowledge the contributions of individual team members.

To build team spirit, it's also important to lead by example. Be a role model for your team, and demonstrate the values and behaviors that you want to see in your employees. Encourage a culture of learning and growth, and provide opportunities for your team to develop their skills and knowledge.

Create opportunities for your team to bond and socialize outside of work. This can help build trust and create a sense of community among your employees. Consider organizing team-building activities, social events, and volunteer opportunities that allow your team to work together towards a common goal.

Ambition

It's important to value ambition in your business. Ambition is about having a clear vision for your business and a strong drive to achieve your goals. It's about pushing yourself to go above and beyond what is expected and taking calculated risks to grow your business and make a positive impact on the world.

To be ambitious, you should set clear and specific goals for your business, both short-term and long-term. These goals should be challenging but achievable and should align with your vision for your business. Set measurable targets and milestones, and track your progress towards achieving them.

To fuel your ambition, you should stay motivated and focused on your goals. Visualize your success and stay positive, even in the face of challenges and setbacks. Surround yourself with supportive people who share your vision and can help you stay motivated and accountable.

At the same time, it's important to be realistic and strategic in pursuing your goals. Take calculated risks and be willing to adapt to changing circumstances. Continuously evaluate your business model and processes to identify areas for improvement and growth.

To be ambitious, you should also be open to learning and growing. Seek out opportunities for professional development and education, and stay up-to-date with the latest industry trends and innovations. Stay curious and open-minded, and be willing to embrace change and innovation.

Positive impact

It's important to consider how your business can create a positive impact on the community and the environment. By integrating social and environmental values into your business practices, you can attract socially conscious customers and employees who share your values and make a positive difference in the world.

To create a positive impact, start by identifying the social or environmental causes that are most important to you and your business. Research the issues and find out how your business can contribute to addressing them. This might involve donating a portion of your profits to a relevant charity, partnering with a local organization, or implementing sustainable business practices that reduce your environmental footprint.

To integrate these values into your business practices, you should start by clearly communicating your values and mission to your customers, employees, and partners. This can help attract socially conscious individuals who share your values and want to support your business. Consider offering incentives to customers and employees who support your social and environmental initiatives, such as discounts or volunteer opportunities.

In addition, you should continuously evaluate and improve your business practices to ensure that they align with your values and create a positive impact. This might involve implementing more sustainable and ethical practices, reducing waste and energy consumption, or supporting local communities and businesses.

Listening

Listening involves actively paying attention to others, seeking to understand their perspectives, and responding with empathy and respect.

To be a good listener, you should create an environment that encourages open communication and feedback. Encourage your team to share their thoughts, concerns, and ideas, and create opportunities for them to do so. This can help foster a sense of trust and respect in the workplace, which can lead to improved collaboration and productivity.

When someone shares their perspective with you, actively listen to what they are saying. This means paying attention to their words, their tone, and their body language and asking questions to clarify anything that you don't understand. Show empathy and respect for their perspective, even if you don't necessarily agree with it.

It's also important to follow through on what you hear from others. If someone raises a concern or offers a suggestion, take it seriously and take steps to address it. This can show your team that you value their input and are committed to creating a positive and productive work environment.

In summary, a successful team has a clearly defined goal and values, effective working methods, a mindset of excellence and mutual respect, and a strong involvement of members in the success of the project.

Chapter 4: Adopting Humanist Leadership

The fourth key to conscious entrepreneurship is adopting humanist leadership. Humanist leadership is a leadership approach that prioritizes the well-being, growth, and development of employees, customers, and stakeholders.

Humanist leaders recognize that a business's success depends not only on its financial performance but also on the satisfaction and fulfillment of the people involved. They aim to create a work environment that promotes trust, respect, and open communication.

....
....
....
....
....
....
....
....
....
....

Who am I?

....
....
....
....
....
....
....
....
....
....

What is my passion?

....
....
....
....
....
....
....
....
....
....

Starting from these questions, we can say that humanism is a philosophy or perspective that values and privileges human beings and human values. The humanist enterprise refers to projects or endeavors that serve humanity and promote its well-being.

At the core of this philosophy is the idea of service - serving our fellow human beings in a spirit of solidarity. This means that a customer is not just a market but a fellow human being; an employee is not just an employee but a fellow human being; and a shareholder is not just a shareholder but a fellow human being. In essence, a human being cannot be a stranger to another human being simply because they are both human.

This philosophy is perhaps best captured in the adage, "Treat others as you would like to be treated." However, recently, we have become so obsessed with economic performance that we have lost sight of this philosophy. We have focused too much on the bottom line, and as a result, we have decentered men in favor of profits.

But it is important to remember that economic performance is ultimately a consequence of our relationships with our customers, collaborators, suppliers, and other stakeholders. By prioritizing service and solidarity, we can build stronger relationships that benefit everyone involved. Unfortunately, our obsession with economic performance is often driven by fear - fear of failure, fear of competition, and fear of losing out. But if we can overcome these fears and recenter our focus on service, we can create a more humane and compassionate world for all.

There are nine fundamental fears:

1. Fear of doing wrong; avoidance process - anger; suggested strategy – perfection

2. Fear of rejection; avoidance process - focusing solely on oneself (our own needs); suggested strategy – service

3. Fear of being worthless; avoidance process - fear of failure; suggested strategy - pursuing success

4. Fear of being without identity; avoidance process - fear of banality; suggested strategy - embracing uniqueness

5. Fear of being incapable; avoidance process - feeling inner emptiness; suggested strategy - seeking knowledge and skills

6. Fear of being betrayed; avoidance process - fear of deviance; suggested strategy - balancing compliance with the rules and healthy skepticism

7. Fear of suffering; avoidance process - avoiding pain and discomfort; suggested strategy - embracing and learning from suffering

8. Fear of being controlled; avoidance process - fear of weakness; suggested strategy - cultivating healthy control and assertiveness

9. Fear of being lost; avoidance process - avoiding conflict; suggested strategy - seeking peace while embracing healthy conflict resolution techniques

By identifying these fundamental fears and understanding their corresponding avoidance processes, we can start to work towards developing healthy strategies for addressing them. We can overcome these fears and cultivate a more fulfilling and meaningful life with awareness and intentional effort.

Humanistic enterprises

Humanistic enterprises recognize their critical role in society as a community that acts for the common good. They emphasize building honest relationships with their suppliers, ensuring high-quality working conditions, both material and relational, and delivering top-notch products and services to their customers.

These companies are highly aware of their economic and social responsibility towards their employees, their ecosystem, and society. They understand that their greatest asset is their people, and they prioritize their well-being above all else.
As a result, humanistic companies are managed by values, not rules. Shared values create team engagement, which is more effective than the obedience engendered by rules. Employees are encouraged to think for themselves, be more productive, autonomous, creative, and, therefore, happier.

Humanistic companies understand that their success is inextricably linked to their employees' success and well-being. They create a virtuous cycle that benefits everyone by treating their employees with respect and dignity, offering fair wages and benefits, and providing a positive working environment.
In addition to their employees, humanistic companies also prioritize their broader social and environmental impact. They strive to minimize their environmental footprint, reduce waste, and engage in sustainable business practices. They also give back to their communities through various philanthropic efforts and social initiatives.

Humanistic enterprises prioritize their societal role, emphasizing their responsibility to their employees, the ecosystem, and the broader community. They are managed by values, not rules, which creates an engaged and productive workforce. They are also committed to minimizing their environmental impact and giving back to their communities, creating a positive social and environmental impact.

The six dimensions of Humanist leadership:

Humanist entrepreneurs embody certain characteristics that set them apart from traditional business leaders:

1. Humanist entrepreneurs see the world as an interdependent and interconnected network of life. They strive to overcome divisions and resolve differences by aligning themselves with a noble cause. By doing so, they change and broaden the perspective of their employees, demonstrating how the company brings solutions to humanity's problems.

2. Humanist entrepreneurs act authentically and appropriately. They strive to align their actions with their convictions, ensuring that their words and behavior coincide with their feelings and wishes. They also adapt their actions to the dynamic context of their company and the wider community.

3. Humanistic entrepreneurs integrate emotions, logic, and intuition into decision-making. They decide with ethical clarity and pragmatism, using their inner compass to identify right or wrong in a given situation. They act cautiously and do not let strong emotions, such as fear or greed, make their decisions. They also know how to listen to their heart, the seat of compassion and intuition. They decide wisely, exercise good judgment in times of crisis, and make ethical and sensible decisions by putting their body, heart, mind, and soul into it.

4. Humanist entrepreneurs have a very clear understanding of their role and lead with humility in any situation. While they prefer to put others in the spotlight and let them shine in times of crisis, they bravely step forward to take the lead and inspire others to follow them.

5. They are undeniably self-aware, allowing their authentic self to shine through and inspire others.

6. Humanist entrepreneurs show "flexible determination." They are motivated to adapt their company's business practices to respond to a changing environment while remaining firmly committed to their social and societal mission. They use their insight, a combination of deep self-awareness, a deep understanding of the past, a lucid perception of the present, and a vision of the future.

7. Humanist entrepreneurs are motivated by "enlightened self-interest." They strive to serve others and invest in a project that serves a noble purpose. They avoid short-term competition and strategies and patiently engage all stakeholders, inside and outside their organization, to co-create sustainable and beneficial value for all actors. They contribute to society as a whole, knowing that by doing so, they will reap the rewards for themselves and their organization.

Benefits of adopting humanist leadership for entrepreneurs:

Improved employee satisfaction and retention: Adopting humanist leadership can significantly impact employee satisfaction and retention. When employees feel valued, respected, and supported, they are more likely to be engaged and committed to their work. This can lead to lower turnover rates and higher levels of employee satisfaction, which can positively impact the business's overall success.

Increased productivity and creativity: Humanist leadership encourages collaboration, communication, and innovation. When employees feel empowered to share their ideas and take ownership of their work, they are more likely to be creative and productive. This can lead to new and innovative ideas that can drive the business's success.

Stronger customer loyalty and trust: Humanist leadership can also positively impact customer loyalty and trust. When employees are happy, engaged, and motivated, they are more likely to provide high-quality products and services that meet or exceed customer expectations. This can lead to higher customer satisfaction, retention, and loyalty.

Positive impact on the bottom line: Adopting humanist leadership can also positively impact the financial success of the business. When employees are satisfied, productive, and engaged, they are more likely to work efficiently and effectively, leading to higher profits and a stronger bottom line. Strong customer loyalty and trust can also lead to increased revenue and profitability over time.

Strategies for implementing humanist leadership in your own business

Encourage open communication and feedback: Creating a work environment where employees feel comfortable expressing their opinions and ideas is essential for humanist leadership. Encourage regular feedback sessions and actively listen to what your employees say. Make sure that all employees have an equal opportunity to share their thoughts and ideas regardless of their position. This approach can help foster a culture of collaboration, innovation, and continuous improvement.

Create a culture of trust and transparency: Building trust with your employees is essential for humanist leadership. Be open and transparent about your business decisions, and communicate your values and vision. Show your employees that you trust and respect them, and empower them to make decisions and take ownership of their work. This approach can help create a positive work culture and community within the organization.

Prioritize employee well-being and development: Humanist leaders prioritize the well-being and development of their employees. This involves providing opportunities for personal and professional growth and promoting work-life balance. Encourage a healthy work environment, and be flexible regarding work schedules and time off. This approach can help foster employee loyalty, reduce turnover, and improve employee satisfaction and productivity.

Lead by example and model humanist leadership principles: As a leader, it's important to lead by example and model the principles you promote. Show your employees that you value and respect them, and prioritize their well-being and development. Be authentic, empathetic, and transparent, and demonstrate a commitment to continuous learning and growth. This approach can help create a positive work culture and shared purpose within the organization.

Chapter 5: Win-win partnership

Thomas Gordon, a psychologist of the humanistic approach, created his first model of conflict resolution (parents-children, teacher-children, then in management). His colleague and friend, Jim Craig, suggested that he use the term "no loss" (NO-LOSS) or "win-win."

A win-win agreement is an agreement whereby each partner is also concerned about the interest of the other in a way that is equally favorable to its interest. It is not a question of seeking the best compromise of sharing gains but of finding an agreement that increases the gains.

In entrepreneurship, you have to know how to create synergies and connections that are in line with your company and your project. We often hear that you need money to start a business; This is wrong; you need an idea that meets a need and know how to group the right people around this idea to realize it.

It is thanks to this thought that I was able to set up my activities. For the first time, I was scammed, and I lost a few thousand euros. What for? A lack of knowledge on the subject, I took a partner at 50-50 so that his company could manage all the administrative parts for me. By hiring a lawyer and a good accountant, I would not have had to make this choice. Nevertheless, this experience was very beneficial. I have acquired knowledge of which I did not know its importance; to know the basics of the laws of the country: on the activity, you carry out (labor law, tax, etc.) have a lawyer as soon as your statute is established and an accountant.

-Renting my first workspace:
The first workspace I found was a garage with a foundation that could support four floors. At that time, I had to have the equivalent of 100 US dollars in my bank account, so I could not afford to pay for a rental. I had projects in progress,

so I went to see the owner and asked him if he could let me access the space so that I start to pay the rent in 1 year with a contract of 10 years, keeping a rent equivalent to the rental of a bedroom apartment in the city and that in return I will build him two floors. By doing the calculations, we were both winners, him in the long term and me in the short term. And I was able to have a workspace without immediate payment.

Opening of my first restaurant without cash flow:
When I opened my first restaurant, I had no cash flow. It was necessary to find people who would be willing to work with a minimum wage while the activity took off. The agreement I made at that time with the employees was that after six months of activity, 25% of the profits would be distributed to them. I announced that two months after the opening of the restaurant, we had to do something to make everyone win. From that day on, the team was motivated! Partners/employees no longer worked for a boss but for them; Flights, delays, absences, and laziness had simply left the team. They were proud and motivated; they gave suggestions for improving the activity. They participated fully in the development of the restaurant. They had before them a new perspective of life.

"We are stronger together" This is true, and I have seen it but with clear, thoughtful and well-organized rules. You can develop a partnership network: with employees, landlords, marketing, and lawyers.
Depending on the form that the partnerships will take, there are multiple advantages. It may even be your new strategic element of development.
Advantages:

Powerful solutions for business growth

When two or more companies come together in a partnership, they bring their own strengths and resources to the table. By working together, they can combine these assets to develop innovative solutions and strategies that can drive business growth. This can include everything from joint product development to shared marketing campaigns, distribution channels, and more.

For example, consider the partnership between Nike and Apple. In 2006, the two companies joined forces to create the Nike+ iPod Sport Kit, which allowed runners to track their workouts using their iPods. This partnership helped both companies achieve their business objectives: Nike was able to reach a new market of tech-savvy consumers, while Apple was able to position the iPod as a must-have accessory for fitness enthusiasts.

Another example is the partnership between Starbucks and PepsiCo. The two companies joined forces to distribute Starbucks ready-to-drink beverages in grocery stores and other retail channels. This partnership allowed Starbucks to expand its reach beyond its physical stores, while PepsiCo was able to tap into the growing demand for premium coffee products.

In both of these examples, the win-win partnership allowed the companies involved to leverage each other's strengths and resources to create powerful solutions for business growth.

Take-off and sustainable development

Another advantage of win-win partnerships is that they can facilitate take-off and sustainable development for businesses. By collaborating with other companies, businesses can access new markets, resources, and expertise that may be difficult to acquire on their own. This can help them achieve rapid growth and ensure sustainable development over the long term.

For instance, consider the partnership between Facebook and PayPal. In 2019, Facebook announced that it would be launching its own cryptocurrency, called Libra (now called Diem). To help facilitate the development of this new payment system, Facebook partnered with PayPal, which would provide payment processing and other financial services. This partnership allowed Facebook to leverage PayPal's extensive network of users and expertise in payment processing, while PayPal was able to tap into Facebook's massive user base and reach.

Similarly, many companies form strategic partnerships with suppliers, distributors, or other businesses in their industry. These partnerships can help companies gain access to new markets, technologies, or resources, and expand their operations both domestically and internationally. By collaborating with other businesses, companies can grow their customer base, increase their revenue, and build a sustainable business model over time.

Complementarity of professions and extension of an offer

Another advantage of win-win partnerships is the complementarity of professions and the extension of the offer. By partnering with other businesses that offer complementary products or services, companies can expand their offering to customers and increase their competitiveness in the market.

For instance, consider the partnership between GoPro and Red Bull. The two companies teamed up to create a platform called "Stratos" that enabled users to capture and share extreme sports videos. GoPro provided the cameras, while Red Bull provided the events and athletes to capture. This partnership allowed both companies to extend their offering and reach a new audience of extreme sports enthusiasts.

Another example is the partnership between Adobe and Microsoft. The two companies have integrated their software offerings to create a seamless workflow for creative professionals. Adobe's Creative Cloud suite can now be used within Microsoft Teams, allowing users to collaborate on projects and share files more easily. This partnership has extended the offering for both companies, allowing them to provide more value to their customers and increase their competitiveness in the market.

In both of these examples, the complementary nature of the businesses involved allowed them to expand their offering to customers and increase their market share. By partnering with other businesses that offer complementary products or services, companies can leverage each other's strengths to create more value for customers and achieve greater success in the market.

Reduction of production, distribution, and marketing costs

By collaborating with other businesses, companies can share the costs of developing and marketing new products or services, reducing the financial burden on each individual company.

For example, imagine a win-win partnership between a software development company and a hardware manufacturer. The software company wants to develop a new application that requires a specific type of hardware, while the hardware manufacturer wants to expand its market by offering new applications that showcase the capabilities of its hardware.

By forming a partnership, the two companies can share the costs of developing and marketing the new application. The software company can leverage the hardware manufacturer's expertise to develop an application that is optimized for the hardware, while the hardware manufacturer can provide the necessary components to make the application work seamlessly on its devices.
Additionally, the two companies can share the marketing costs of promoting the new application. By leveraging each other's marketing channels and resources, they can reach a broader audience and reduce the costs of promoting the application to potential customers.

The win-win partnership between the software development company and the hardware manufacturer reduces the production, distribution, and marketing costs for both companies. By working together, they can share the costs of developing and marketing a new product, while also leveraging each other's expertise and resources to create a product that is optimized for their target market.

In conclusion, win-win partnerships offer businesses the opportunity to collaborate with other companies to leverage each other's strengths, expand offerings, and increase competitiveness in the market. By working together, businesses can overcome limitations, reduce costs, and achieve sustainable growth. Embracing a collaborative approach and opening up to partnerships can drive innovation and lead to greater success in the market.

Chapter 6: KNOW EACH OTHER

One of the key aspects of conscious entrepreneurship is the importance of self-awareness and knowing oneself. Understanding your values, strengths, weaknesses, and unique qualities is essential for developing a clear vision and direction for your business.

Carl Jung, the Swiss psychologist and student of Sigmund Freud, believed that self-knowledge was fundamental to understanding human nature and avoiding the dangers of our psychology. He developed psychological profiles highlighting differences in personality traits and how people process information to make decisions. For example, he identified extroverts and introverts, sensory and intuitive types, and those who rely on feeling or reasoning to make decisions.

As an entrepreneur, it is crucial to be aware of your tendencies and preferences in decision-making. This knowledge can help you manage the pressure and responsibilities of running a business and ensure that your actions are aligned with your values and purpose. Taking time to assess your mental health and well-being is also essential for the long-term sustainability of your activities.

To develop a deeper understanding of yourself as a conscious entrepreneur, consider practicing meditation, journaling, and seeking feedback from trusted colleagues or mentors. Reflect on your own experiences and values, and how they can guide your decision-making and vision for your business. By knowing yourself, you can better navigate the challenges and opportunities of entrepreneurship with clarity and purpose.

The Importance of Self-Knowledge in Entrepreneurship

Self-knowledge is a critical component of entrepreneurship and can significantly impact the success of a conscious entrepreneur. In a fast-paced and competitive business environment, entrepreneurs face numerous challenges, including pressure, ambiguity, and uncertainty. Self-knowledge can help entrepreneurs navigate these challenges and maintain their well-being, stability, and sustainability in the long run.

Firstly, self-knowledge helps entrepreneurs identify their strengths and weaknesses, enabling them to focus on what they do best and delegate tasks that may not be in their area of expertise. Understanding personal tendencies and limitations also help to avoid potential pitfalls and failures.

Secondly, self-knowledge contributes to the development of an effective leadership style. Entrepreneurs who understand their personality traits, communication style, and decision-making preferences can lead authentically, effectively communicate with their team, and make decisions that align with their values.

Thirdly, self-knowledge promotes emotional intelligence, allowing entrepreneurs to manage their emotions, handle stress, and cultivate positive relationships with their team, clients, and stakeholders. It also facilitates self-reflection and self-awareness, enabling entrepreneurs to continually evaluate their actions and make improvements.

Finally, self-knowledge helps entrepreneurs establish a sense of purpose and meaning, which is essential for conscious entrepreneurship. By understanding their values and aspirations, entrepreneurs can develop a vision that aligns with their personal goals and contributes positively to society and the environment.

Where are you with your:
Ability to love life? (Are you happy)

....
....
....
....
....
....

....
....

....
....

-Resilience? (your ability to adjust to the unexpected and start anew) ....

....
....

....
....

....
....

....
....

-       Balance? (give yourself time for family, friends, and yourself)

....
....

....
....

....
....

....
....

....
....

-       Personal fulfillment? (Where are you with the list of what you would like
to learn and do?)

....
....

....
....

....
....

....
....
....
....

-        Flexibility? (how do you deal with bad news?)
....
....
....
....
....
....
....
....
....
....

Take time to ask yourself the essential questions, and use them as a compass that will show us the path to take through life's journey.

I started entrepreneurship very young, boosted by a desire to solve the family's financial problems to find a union. A mad rush to work. In 2014, I managed five entrepreneurial activities: I thought "company", lived "company", and breathed "company "; nothing could stop me; until the day when, for some other reason, I decided to go to therapy. The psychologist told me that all the energy I put into my professional activities was directed by the powerful engine of escaping the traumas of the past and that it was time to put everything flat to build a stable life. One year was the time it took me to understand the reasons that drove me to work tirelessly, define sustainable goals over time, and understand my priorities to serve the community better. It was a difficult but crucial step that allowed me to know myself in-depth and how to direct my life and find what I was made for. A simple tool, I was no longer in the automatic pilotage that life imposed on me; I could finally take control of myself; without stress, anxiety, anxiety due to all the fears in me, I was finally FREE!

This freedom allowed me to clean up my life; I knew precisely what I wanted to do and what I would no longer allow being done to me. I was no longer working like a robot; I was out of the matrix and had a clear and precise vision of who I am and want to accomplish in the long term.

And there, a miracle came to me; I was aligned with my destiny, and the more I advanced, the more precise the professional project became.

By doing therapy, self-therapy, an inner retrospection, you become aware of who you are and what you can accomplish without being drained by your fears but by your serene forces and open up to the world, to sharing, to connections to realize your projects.

Understanding Your Personality Type

Understanding your personality type is an important part of self-knowledge in entrepreneurship. The famous psychologist Carl Jung identified several personality types that are still widely used today. Two of the most important distinctions are between introverts and extroverts.
Introverts are people who draw energy from their inner world and can find social interactions draining. Extroverts, on the other hand, draw energy from their external environment and thrive on social interactions.

Another important distinction is between sensory and intuitive types. Sensory types primarily use their five senses to gather information and make decisions based on that information. On the other hand, intuitive types are more likely to rely on their instincts to gather information and make decisions.

Finally, there is a distinction between thinking and feeling types. Thinking types make decisions based on logic and reason, while feeling types make decisions based on emotions and values.

Understanding your personality type can be useful in entrepreneurship because it can help you understand your strengths and weaknesses and how you approach problem-solving. It can also help you understand how you interact with others and how to work with people who have different personality types.

The Role of Self-Awareness in Entrepreneurial Success

Self-awareness plays a critical role in the success of an entrepreneur. By understanding their personality type, an entrepreneur can better manage their emotions and tendencies and make decisions aligned with their values and strengths. This awareness can also help entrepreneurs cope with pressure and responsibilities, as they can recognize when they feel overwhelmed and take steps to address their mental health.

In addition, self-awareness can help entrepreneurs identify and address areas for personal and professional development and help them build a strong support network. By understanding their strengths and weaknesses, entrepreneurs can build a team with complementary skills and experiences and develop relationships with mentors and advisors who can provide guidance and support.

Chapter 7: The art of creating Connections

Entrepreneurs have the natural ability to make connections. They are good communicators, which helps them convey their ideas clearly.

It doesn't matter where you work or the position you have; The art of knowing how to make a connection can open up many possibilities for you. This is an essential skill for success. Relationships are never acquired; they are built, developed by sharing common affinities and preserved in loyalty. It is by creating relationships that we establish trust, which allows others to open up to you, share information, buy your products, recommend your company, and support your ideas.

Note that you are not alone and that if you want to move forward in your projects, connections are essential. If you want to start making connections, here are some ways to go about it.

Use open-ended questions to get to know the person

One effective way to make connections is to use open-ended questions to get to know the person you are speaking with. Open-ended questions encourage conversation and allow the person to give more than a simple yes or no response.

When using open-ended questions, it is important to be genuine and show a sincere interest in the person's experiences, opinions, and ideas. This will help to build trust and rapport between you and the person you are speaking with.

Examples of open-ended questions include:

- "Can you tell me more about your background and how you got into this industry?"
- "What are some struggles you have faced in your business, and how did you overcome them?"

- "What are some of your favorite projects you have worked on and why?"
- "What innovations in the industry excite you?"

By asking open-ended questions, you can learn more about the person you are speaking with and establish a deeper connection. This can also help you identify potential opportunities for collaboration or partnerships in the future. Remember to actively listen to their responses and use follow-up questions to continue the conversation and show your interest in what they have to say.

Find a topic that interests the other.

When trying to make connections as an entrepreneur, finding a topic that interests the other person can be a great way to start a conversation and build a connection. By showing an interest in the other person's passions and interests, you can demonstrate that you value their perspectives and opinions.

To find a topic that interests the other person, try to learn more about them by asking questions or doing some research. You can look at their social media profiles or website to see what they post about or what projects they have worked on in the past. You can also ask mutual acquaintances for information or suggestions.

Once you have identified a topic that the other person is passionate about, use it to start a conversation. For example, if the person is involved in a nonprofit organization, ask them about the work they do and what motivated them to get involved. If they are a musician, ask them about their creative process and how they got started in the industry.

Remember that it is important to be genuine and show a sincere interest in the topic. Avoid faking interest or asking questions just for the sake of conversation, as this can come across as insincere or manipulative.

By finding a topic that interests the other person, you can create a meaningful connection and potentially identify opportunities for collaboration or partnership in the future.

Be empathetic

By understanding the other person's perspective and experiences, you can build a stronger connection and establish a sense of trust and mutual understanding.

To be empathetic:

1. Try to listen actively and pay attention to the other person's verbal and nonverbal cues.
2. Show that you are genuinely interested in what they have to say by asking follow-up questions and reflecting on their responses.
3. Try to put yourself in their position and imagine how you would feel in their situation.

Being empathetic also involves showing respect for the other person's feelings and experiences, even if you don't necessarily agree with them. Avoid being judgmental or dismissive, and try to approach the conversation with an open mind and a willingness to learn.

In addition to building stronger connections, being empathetic can also help you identify opportunities for collaboration or partnership by understanding the other person's goals and priorities. By showing that you value their perspective and experiences, you can build a foundation for a mutually beneficial relationship.

Develop your emotional intelligence.

Emotional intelligence (EI) is the ability to recognize and understand your own emotions, as well as the emotions of others, and use this information to guide your thinking and behavior.

To develop emotional intelligence, start by becoming more aware of your own emotions and reactions. Pay attention to how you feel in different situations, and try to identify patterns in your emotional responses. This can help you gain a better understanding of your own emotional triggers and how they influence your thoughts and actions.

Next, practice actively listening to others and paying attention to their emotional cues. This means not just hearing what they say but also observing their body language, tone of voice, and other nonverbal cues. This can help you gain insight into how others feel and what their thoughts may be, even if they don't express them directly.

Another key aspect of developing emotional intelligence is learning how to regulate your own emotions. This means being able to manage your own feelings and reactions in a way that is appropriate and productive. For example, if you feel angry or frustrated, you might take a few deep breaths or step away from the situation to calm down before responding.

Finally, developing emotional intelligence also involves using your emotional awareness and regulation skills to connect with others. This means being able to recognize and respond to the emotions of others in a way that is compassionate and empathetic. By demonstrating empathy and understanding, you can build stronger connections with others and establish a foundation for a successful partnership or collaboration.

Adapt to the language of the other:

Adapting to the language of the other person is an important aspect of making connections as an entrepreneur. It involves being aware of the other person's communication style and adjusting your own language and tone to match theirs.

One way to adapt to the other person's language is to pay attention to the level of complexity in their speech. If the other person is using simple language, it can be helpful to use simple language as well. This can make it easier for them to understand and relate to what you're saying, which can help build rapport and understanding.

If the other person is using more complex language, it can be beneficial to use more sophisticated language in your own communication. This can demonstrate that you understand their perspective and are capable of engaging in more nuanced discussions.

It's important to note that adapting to the language of the other person doesn't mean sacrificing your own communication style or dumbing down your ideas. Rather, it's about finding common ground and using language that is accessible and relatable to the other person.

In addition to language, it's also important to be aware of cultural differences in communication styles. Different cultures may have different norms around directness, formality, and nonverbal communication, so it's important to be sensitive to these differences and adapt your communication accordingly.

Be sincere

Being sincere is an essential component of making connections as an entrepreneur. It means being honest and authentic in your interactions with others and avoiding the temptation to put on a false persona or exaggerate your accomplishments.

Being sincere involves being genuine and transparent in your communication, both verbally and nonverbally. This means expressing your thoughts and feelings honestly and avoiding any attempts to mislead or deceive the other person. It also means being open to feedback and willing to admit when you've made a mistake or don't know the answer to a question.

Sincerity is important because it helps build trust and credibility with others. When people feel that you are honest, they can trust your judgment and expertise and be willing to work with you on future projects or collaborations.

On the other hand, insincerity can quickly erode trust and damage relationships. If people feel that you are not being honest or that you are putting on a false front, they may be hesitant to work with you or recommend you to others.

In conclusion, in today's competitive business world, making connections is a vital skill for entrepreneurs looking to grow their businesses and make an impact in their field. By building strong relationships with others, entrepreneurs can gain valuable insights, access new opportunities for collaboration and growth, and build a network of supporters who can help them achieve their goals.

Chapter 8: Continuing Education

Continuing education has become increasingly important in today's rapidly changing and competitive world. As industries evolve and new technologies emerge, keeping pace with the latest advancements in your field of activity is essential. Simply earning a diploma or degree is no longer enough to guarantee success in your career. To remain relevant, you must be willing to invest time and effort into ongoing learning and development.

By actively seeking out opportunities to improve your skills and knowledge, you can stay up-to-date with the latest industry developments and demonstrate your dedication and commitment to your profession. Continuing education can provide various benefits, from improving your performance and boosting your career prospects to discovering new interests and opportunities to stand out.

In this fast-paced and ever-changing world, those who are proactive and committed to lifelong learning are better positioned to succeed. By continuously seeking new skills and knowledge, you can remain competitive and adaptable and open doors to new opportunities. With access to an abundance of information and resources available through online training, workshops, and professional associations, there are endless opportunities to develop new skills and take your career to the next level.

The new skills acquired make it possible to:
Improve performance: Continuously learning and acquiring new skills can help you become more efficient, productive, and effective in your role. You can apply your new knowledge to your current job responsibilities, allowing you to perform your job better, more confidently, and more efficiently. This can lead to improved performance, increased productivity, and greater job satisfaction.

Boost your career: With the job market becoming increasingly competitive, it's essential to remain relevant and up-to-date with the latest industry developments. Continuously developing your skills and knowledge can help you stand out from other candidates and make you a more attractive candidate for promotions and career advancement opportunities. Investing in your ongoing education and development can expand your skill set and increase your value to employers, which can lead to more significant career opportunities and increased earning potential.

Discover new interests: Pursuing continuing education can allow exploring new interests and passions. Whether taking courses in a new field or attending a workshop to learn a new skill, continuous learning can be a great way to expand your horizons and discover new passions. This can help you maintain a sense of personal fulfillment and engagement, which can translate into greater job satisfaction and overall happiness.

To stand out: In today's competitive job market, standing out from the crowd is essential. By continuously developing your skills and knowledge, you can differentiate yourself from others and become a more attractive candidate for employers. Demonstrating a commitment to lifelong learning and professional development can indicate to employers that you are dedicated to your profession, willing to go the extra mile, and have a strong work ethic. This can make you a more appealing candidate for promotions and new career opportunities.

How to develop new skills?

Learn from those who succeed: By rubbing shoulders with experts in your field of activity, you will be more efficient and competent.
Take 5-10 minutes of your time every day to learn a new skill. It's an invaluable investment! Search and inform yourself continuously; today, we have access to all information and online training.

Engage in experiential learning: To enhance your skills, engage in experiential learning by taking on new challenges, assignments, or projects that require you to use and develop your skills. This can help you to apply your skills in new contexts and gain valuable experience.

Attend workshops and training sessions: Attend workshops and training sessions to learn new skills and gain exposure to new technologies or methodologies. These can be offered through your employer, industry associations, or online training platforms.

Join a professional organization: Join a professional organization in your field to gain access to industry-specific resources, networking opportunities, and training programs. These can provide opportunities to learn from experts, attend conferences, and build your professional network.

Take online courses: Enroll in online courses offered by reputable institutions or platforms to learn new skills, gain knowledge, and earn credentials. Online courses are convenient, flexible, and often more affordable than traditional classroom-based courses.

Read industry publications and blogs: Stay up-to-date with the latest trends and best practices in your field by regularly reading industry publications, blogs, and forums. These can provide valuable insights into emerging technologies, industry developments, and thought leadership.

Practice, practice, practice: To develop and hone your skills, practice regularly. This can be achieved through simulation exercises, role-playing, or real-life scenarios. By practicing regularly, you can build confidence and proficiency in your skills.

Recognize the importance of continuing education: In today's fast-paced and ever-changing world, ongoing learning is essential to keep up with the latest trends, technologies, and best practices in your field of activity. Acknowledge that a diploma is no longer enough, and commit to lifelong learning.

Set clear goals: Define your learning objectives and determine the skills, knowledge, and competencies you need to acquire or enhance to achieve your career aspirations. This will help you to focus your efforts and make informed decisions about the learning opportunities you pursue.

Identify your learning style: Determine your preferred learning style, visual, auditory, or kinesthetic. Knowing your learning style can help you to choose the most effective learning strategies and methods that align with your natural learning preferences.

Seek out diverse learning opportunities: Explore various learning opportunities, such as workshops, conferences, online courses, and mentorship programs. Seek opportunities that align with your learning objectives and offer diverse perspectives and experiences.

Network with experts and peers: Connect with professionals in your field of activity, both in-person and online, to expand your knowledge and gain insights into the latest trends and best practices. Collaborating with peers can also provide opportunities for peer-to-peer learning and skill-sharing.

Make time for learning: Dedicate a regular learning schedule, whether a few minutes each day or several hours per week. This will help you stay on track and progress towards your learning goals.

Evaluate your progress: Regularly assess and adjust your learning strategies as needed. This will help you stay focused, motivated, and progress towards your learning objectives.

Apply what you learn: Finally, apply what you learn to your work or personal life. This can help you to enhance your performance, improve your problem-solving skills, and bring new ideas and perspectives to your work or personal life. Additionally, consider sharing your new skills or knowledge with colleagues or peers, which can create opportunities for mentorship and knowledge-sharing.

Continuing education is an important aspect of personal and professional growth. However, pursuing continuous learning can be challenging for many individuals due to time constraints, financial barriers, and lack of motivation. This section will explore strategies for overcoming these obstacles and making ongoing education more accessible.

Strategies for Overcoming Time Constraints

A lack of time is the most common obstacle to continuous learning. Many individuals have busy schedules with work, family, and other commitments. However, several strategies can help overcome time constraints, including:

Creating a schedule: Planning your time can help you stay on track and make the most of your available time. Consider using a planner, calendar, or scheduling app to keep yourself organized.

Prioritizing tasks: When you have limited time, it's important to prioritize tasks based on their importance and urgency. Focus on high-priority tasks first and leave lower-priority tasks for later.

Take advantage of downtime: Look for learning opportunities during your daily routine. For example, you could listen to educational podcasts or audiobooks during your commute or while exercising.

Strategies for Overcoming Financial Barriers

Another common obstacle to pursuing continuous learning is financial barriers. Many educational programs and courses can be expensive, making it difficult for some individuals to access them. However, several strategies can help overcome financial barriers, including:

Seeking out free or low-cost resources: There are many educational resources available for free or at a low cost, such as online courses, webinars, and educational videos. Look for opportunities to learn without breaking the bank.

Applying for scholarships or grants: Many educational programs and institutions offer scholarships or grants to help students cover the cost of tuition and other expenses. Research these opportunities and apply for any that you may be eligible for.

Negotiating with your employer: If you're pursuing continuing education to advance your career, consider asking your employer to cover the cost of your education. Many employers offer tuition reimbursement programs or other educational benefits for their employees.

Strategies for Overcoming Lack of Motivation

A lack of motivation can also be an obstacle to pursuing continuous learning. It's easy to become discouraged or overwhelmed when faced with the prospect of acquiring new skills or knowledge. However, several strategies can help overcome a lack of motivation, including:

Setting achievable goals: Break your learning goals into smaller, achievable ones. Celebrate your successes along the way to help you stay motivated.

Finding a support system: Surround yourself with individuals who support your goals and can help hold you accountable. Joining a study group or seeking out a mentor can also be helpful.

Staying curious: Cultivate a sense of curiosity and a passion for learning. Stay engaged with your field of interest by attending conferences, reading industry publications, and participating in online forums.

In conclusion, continuous learning is a crucial aspect of personal and professional growth, but it can be challenging to stay motivated and focused without a clear plan. Setting achievable goals is an effective way to stay on track and measure progress. By breaking down larger learning objectives into smaller, manageable steps, individuals can build momentum and stay motivated to continue their education.

Another strategy for overcoming obstacles to continuing education is to seek support from mentors or peers. Whether through formal mentorship programs or informal networking, having access to knowledgeable and experienced individuals can provide valuable guidance and support. Peers can also provide motivation and accountability, helping individuals stay on track with their learning goals.

Leveraging technology and online resources is another way to make continuous learning more accessible. With the rise of online learning platforms, individuals have access to a wealth of resources, including courses, tutorials, and articles, all at their fingertips. Technology can also help individuals stay organized, track progress, and connect with other learners and experts in their field.

Overall, the importance of continuous learning cannot be overstated, and with the right strategies in place, individuals can overcome common obstacles and achieve their educational and career goals.

Conclusion

In this book, we have explored the eight key principles of conscious entrepreneurship. These principles include having a clear understanding of your canvas, creating a compelling vision, focusing on value, adopting humanistic leadership, forming win-win partnerships, cultivating self-awareness, mastering the art of making connections, and committing to continuous education.

By following these principles, you can build successful businesses that prioritize the common good. They can create products and services that are both profitable and sustainable, while also benefiting society and the environment.

Conscious entrepreneurs understand that their role in society is to serve a larger purpose than just making money. They prioritize the well-being of their employees, their communities, and the planet. They lead with empathy, compassion, and self-awareness, inspiring their teams to be more creative, autonomous, and productive.

Conscious entrepreneurs also understand the power of collaboration and partnership, seeking out opportunities to work with like-minded individuals and organizations to achieve shared goals. They are continuously learning, adapting, and evolving, seeking out new knowledge and skills to improve themselves and their businesses.

In summary, conscious entrepreneurship is about more than just making a profit. It is about creating businesses that are aligned with a larger purpose and that prioritize the well-being of all stakeholders. By following the eight key principles outlined in this e-book, entrepreneurs can build successful, sustainable, and socially responsible businesses that make a positive impact on the world.

www.ingramcontent.com/pod-product-compliance
Lightning Source LLC
Chambersburg PA
CBHW070749220526
45467CB00018B/1710